COUNCIL *on*
FOREIGN
RELATIONS

Center for Preventive Action

Discussion Paper Series on Managing Global Disorder No. 11
November 2022

Climate Change and Conflict in the Sahel

Beza Tesfaye

This Discussion Paper was made possible by a grant from the Carnegie Corporation of New York. The statements made and views expressed are solely the responsibility of the author.

CONTENTS

INTRODUCTION

The link between climate change and conflict is increasingly at the fore-front of security and development discussions as evidence continues to mount of the far-reaching effects of climate change on various aspects of human life. One place of greatest concern is the Sahel, a region defined by challenging environmental conditions.

The Sahel, which means "border" in Arabic, is a geographic region in Africa separating the Sahara Desert in the north from the tropics to the south.[1] Two thousand six hundred miles long and six hundred miles at its widest, the Sahel is predominantly characterized by arid and semi-arid lands, which average twelve to twenty inches of rain per year.[2] The western Sahel is commonly understood as the six francophone countries in West Africa—Burkina Faso, Chad, Mali, Mauritania, Niger, and Senegal—that are collectively home to more than one hundred million people.[3] Two axes of instability exist in this region: the Liptako-Gourma area at the borderlands between Burkina Faso, Mali, and Niger, and the Lake Chad Basin, which stretches across Chad, Niger, and Nigeria.

Since the 2000s, the Sahel has been a prime focus of counterter-rorism and stabilization efforts by the United States and Europe. Yet, despite multiple military interventions and billions of dollars in security assistance, violent conflicts involving jihadi insurgencies and intercom-munal violence have steadily increased over the past decade, claiming tens of thousands of lives, displacing more than 2.5 million people within the region, and placing many more in need of humanitarian assistance.[4] As instability grows and begins to spill over to coastal West African countries, policymakers in the United States and Europe are now looking beyond proximate causes to understand the structural and local drivers of conflict and fragility, including environmental factors.

Climate change predictions indicate that increasing temperatures and more frequent weather extremes will continue to hit the Sahel region harder than other parts of the world. Populations that inhabit the region have, in the past, adapted in various ways to environmental hardships, but the confluence of evolving economic, political, and social factors, coupled with the momentum of environmental shifts, presents new risks. Climate change and conflict interact differently depending on context. In the Sahel, climate change can be viewed as an indirect "threat multiplier" that compounds the many local risk factors for conflict. Changing patterns of migration are among those risk factors, though mobility has long been a coping mechanism employed by Sahelian communities faced with environmental hardship.[5] Overreliance on climate-sensitive, agriculture-based livelihoods is also a risk factor in the Sahel. Overuse of water and land reduces resource availability over time; as agricultural production falters due to climate variability, food prices increase as food security declines. This phenomenon raises the risk of collective violence.[6]

These challenges could lead to heightened levels of deprivation and insecurity; the ability of Sahelian countries to manage these risks will depend on local, national, regional, and international responses. Conflict in the Sahel is primarily rooted in political and governance-related weaknesses. Likewise, effective governance can mitigate and prevent climate-related conflict. For example, Morocco, Sudan, and Syria, all agriculture-dependent countries prone to destructive droughts, have had vastly different experiences with climate-related conflict. Unlike Sudan and Syria, Morocco has largely been able to avoid internal conflict due to government policies that protected domestic producers and helped rural communities avoid food insecurity.[7] A proper recognition of the role that governance and policy play in shaping peace and security is crucial for framing climate security challenges in the Sahel, where institutional weaknesses are as formidable as environmental hardships.

Climate change can also act to multiply threats of grave concern to the United States and the West. In the Sahel, those threats include the spread of violent extremism, growing demand for international aid, and the proliferation of weak, authoritarian governance. The United States would be well served to implement policies that try to tackle these issues through international cooperation and promote a more resilient and stable Sahel.

CONTEXTUAL FACTORS AND TRENDS

Sahelian countries are simultaneously among the most affected by climate change and the least prepared to adapt. It is commonly noted that Africa is warming faster than the global average, but within Africa, the Sahel has seen the largest average temperature increases.[8] At the same time, five of the six Sahelian countries are in the bottom twenty-five of the Notre Dame Global Adaptation Initiative Country Index, which ranks countries based on their vulnerability to climate change and readiness to improve resilience.[9]

Further complicating the region's environmental challenges, the Sahel continues to face significant development obstacles. Sahelian countries rank among the lowest in the world on the UN Human Development Index, and extreme poverty remains prevalent. The region has made incremental gains in per capita income and life expectancy since the 1990s, driven by economic growth, which has averaged 4.8 percent per year since 2010. Nonetheless, 80 percent of the population lives on less than $2 per day.

In recent decades, the Sahel has struggled with high levels of political instability, state fragility, and conflict. Chad, Mali, and Niger are ranked among the bottom twenty-five on the Fragile States Index, with Mauritania and Burkina Faso scoring only slightly higher.[10] Senegal is the only one of the six countries that has been relatively peaceful, democratic, and stable in its postcolonial period. Three countries in particular—Burkina Faso, Mali, and Niger—have been embroiled in a complex and interconnected security crisis, the epicenter of which is in Mali, where an armed insurgency began in 2012. Widespread discontent with governments, the fallout from continued insecurity as well as poorly managed social challenges, has enabled multiple military coups in Mali and Burkina Faso (along with a failed attempt in Niger). Those political challenges have also allowed local grievances to fester and be exploited by a growing array of armed nonstate actors.

ENVIRONMENTAL CONTEXT

A series of droughts beginning in the late 1960s and lasting through the mid-1990s demonstrates the Sahel's vulnerability to adverse climate events. During that period, the Sahel experienced a 30 percent decrease in rainfall compared with the 1950s.[11] Cyclical periods of rainfall variability are characteristic of the region, but no other part of the world has experienced as large a change in the twentieth century as the Sahel over the same period.[12] At the peak of the disaster in 1973, experts estimated that more than one hundred thousand people died due to famine.[13] Droughts have also been credited for drastic ecological changes such as the shrinking of Lake Chad and a reduction in plant cover linked to desertification.[14] In response to those crises, large numbers of people have moved from northern regions of the Sahel to the south, particularly to coastal countries in West Africa.[15]

Since the 1990s, environmental conditions have improved but continue to be precarious. Rainfall levels have returned to their historical average, and experts note a pattern of "regreening" in areas that had been affected by drought.[16] However, in recent decades, two notable weather trends have emerged. The first is higher temperatures, including heat waves that have become longer and hotter. Specifically, the average surface temperature in West Africa has increased by 1°C to 3°C (a difference of 3.6°F) since the mid-1970s, with the highest increase recorded in the Sahel.[17] The second trend is increasing but more variable rainfall, which has led to severe flooding.[18] For example, the 2020 rainy season recorded the highest rainfall total in twenty years in the Sahel.[19] The unexpected amount of precipitation led to devastating floods. Across Niger, at least 45 people were killed, 226,000 were displaced, and close to 10,000 hectares of crops were destroyed.[20] Like 2020, the 2021 rainy season recorded average to above average rainfall but started and ended earlier than normal. The World Food Program notes that "the poor temporal distribution of rains is likely to have had a negative effect on crop and pasture development."[21] Altogether, the recent environmental trends—prolonged heat and dryness coupled with shorter, more intense rainfall periods—spell trouble for the region.

SOCIOECONOMIC CONTEXT

Owing to limited economic development, the economies of most Sahelian countries still rely on the exploitation of natural resources. Eighty percent of the Sahel's population practices subsistence agriculture (including pastoralism) and fishing—livelihoods that are highly sensitive to fluctuations in environmental conditions.[22] For example, since the 1960s, periods of drought and variability in rainfall patterns have contributed to a 34 percent reduction in agricultural productivity in Africa.[23] Because the vast majority of agriculture in the Sahel is rain fed (only 5 percent of land is irrigated), households are at risk in the event of failure or poor distribution of rain during the single rainy season each year.[24] As a result, communities have adopted techniques to spread their risk, such as planting crops with diverse maturation times, water needs, and uses (i.e., commercial versus for consumption) to maximize returns.[25]

In this context, seasonal migration is often an important source of income diversification. In places such as Mali and Niger, able-bodied men migrate during the dry season and return at the beginning of the rainy season to help prepare farms for the yearly harvest.[26] This periodic movement typically brings migrants to urban areas or to more developed neighboring countries, particularly Ghana, Ivory Coast, Nigeria, and Senegal. The establishment of the Economic Community of West African States (ECOWAS) in 1975 supported and formalized free movement across Sahelian and West African states. Though often employed in the informal sector, successful migrants can support their households by sending remittances, creating a cycle of interdependence between hard-to-inhabit rural areas and towns and cities.[27] This manner of seasonal migration can be viewed as a long-standing adaptation strategy to environmental hardship.[28]

However, the sustainability of livelihoods and social relations in the Sahel is coming under increasing pressure. Livelihoods often correspond with ethnicity, with groups such as the Bambara, Hausa, Songhai, and Zarma associated with farming, and others such as the Tuareg and Fulani associated with nomadic herding (although practicing both is increasingly common). For centuries, farmers and herders have peacefully shared natural resources. Pastoralists typically move their herds from north to south during the dry season in search of pasture and water, and traditionally exchange manure and milk for grazing access.[29] In recent years, this system of cooperation has diminished as agricultural land expands at the expense of pasture.[30] Satellite images reveal that between 1975 and 2013, the percentage of land in West Africa being cultivated doubled from 10.7 percent to 22.4 percent, replacing savannas used for grazing, as well as wetlands and forests.[31] The reason for this change is twofold.

First, rapid population growth, which averages about 3 percent annually, is increasing demand for land in rural areas. [32] Second, at the same time, land productivity in the Sahel has declined because of both climate change and unsustainable practices leading to land degradation.[33] Faced with declining yields, farmers have sought more land to sustain themselves. Agricultural encroachment on traditional rangelands—and inversely the problem of cattle grazing on cropland—has triggered a growing number of clashes between farmers and herders over land and water resources necessary for both groups' survival.

Land tenure systems contribute an additional dimension of complexity to resource-based conflicts in the Sahel. The foundation of many existing tenure systems is rooted in customary land practices from precolonial periods. States have updated and codified requirements for land ownership during the colonial and postcolonial eras, but discrepancies between recent statutory tenure and older customary tenure policies are not uncommon. For example, in Mali, although statutory laws recognize the state's rights to acquire and utilize unused lands based on the French principle of *mise en valeur* (enhancement or development), customary systems recognize the authority of customary entities over traditional cultural lands, including pasturelands. Attempts to harmonize disparate laws and customary practices to adjudicate land tenure disputes are occurring, but they lack transparency and consistency. Rent-seeking practices employed by local state officials to exploit people and communities during land disputes contribute to land insecurity and grievances.

Relatedly, government economic policies favoring large-scale agricultural development have threatened traditional ways of life. Both herders and farmers have lost land to commercial agriculture projects, irrigation schemes, and the construction of dams, often with insufficient compensation. However, agrarian modernization has come at the particular expense of pastoralists who have been pressured to give up their mobile lifestyle, leading to a sense of group marginalization.

POLITICAL CONTEXT

Sahelian governments have faced formidable challenges providing services as well as law and order in peripheral areas, especially given that many of the countries are geographically expansive with highly rural populations.[34] Limited state presence in these peripheries has contributed both to the marginalization of certain groups, such as the Tuareg that inhabit northern Mali and Niger, and to the growth of illicit economies, including the trafficking of goods, drugs, and migrants by opportunistic actors. Recent insurgencies have only exacerbated these governance challenges by further limiting government access and control of remote areas.

The emergence of the ongoing security crisis in the Sahel can be linked to weaknesses in state capacity coupled with government corruption and ineffective policies. Although Mali was externally praised in the 2000s as an exemplar of democracy in West Africa, internal corruption and rent-seeking undermined the presidency of Amadou Toumani Touré. By 2012, an insurgency in the north led by thousands of heavily armed Tuareg soldiers returning from Libya after the fall of President Muammar al-Qaddafi, along with al-Qaeda-affiliated Islamist groups from Algeria, exposed the state's weaknesses and led to a military coup.[35] Over time, a military operation assisted by French troops pushed the insurgents back from occupying large swaths of Mali's northern regions of Kidal, Gao, and Tombouctou. In 2015, a peace agreement was signed between the Malian government, pro-government militias, and a coalition of Tuareg rebel groups—though excluding jihadi groups—to end the fighting. Yet, security has continued to deteriorate despite these gains, with conflict-related deaths steadily increasing since 2016 as the insurgency spread to Burkina Faso and Niger.[36] Currently, the greatest threats emanating from the region, particularly in the tri-border Liptako-Gourma area, are the al-Qaeda-affiliated Jama'at Nasr al-Islam wal Muslimin (JNIM) and the Islamic State in the Greater Sahara.[37]

The success of these transnational jihadi groups across the Sahel owes more to ongoing state failures than to ideological support. Public opinion polls in Burkina Faso, Mali, and Niger indicate high levels of dissatisfaction with government performance, including in addressing unemployment and corruption.[38] Insurgent groups capitalize on those frustrations and gain support by establishing alternative systems of local governance. For example, when government forces are unable or unwilling to provide security in remote areas, insurgent groups position themselves as defenders of local populations against criminality and banditry.[39] Scholars Tor Benjaminsen and Boubacar Ba have chronicled how insurgents have been able to "win [the] hearts and minds" of Fulani pastoralists in central Mali by more effectively addressing land disputes than local government officials who accept bribes to stall adjudication.[40]

The militarized response to the insurgency represents another state failure. Thousands of foreign and national forces have been deployed to fight the insurgents. The counterinsurgency measures have led to an alarming rate of human rights abuses and an atmosphere of impunity. In 2020, security forces were responsible for more civilian fatalities in Burkina Faso and Mali than violent extremist groups or communal violence.[41]

Insecurity and state fragility have created a new normal of instability in the Sahel, particularly in the peripheries where conflicts are driven by uneven development and weak governance. Jason Stearns, the founder of the Congo Research Group at New York University's Center on International Cooperation, notes that in similar conflicts armed insurgents are not trying to capture state control, but rather act as "violence perpetrators" that "seek to extract resources from the state and local residents, involve themselves in local governance and offer young men . . . a means of survival and dignity."[42] Although the violence in the Sahel is often characterized as a low-intensity conflict in comparison with conventional wars, it continues to feed on and devastate marginal communities with no end in sight.

EMERGING RISKS AND ANTICIPATED EFFECTS

A confluence of crises has radically transformed the Sahel over the past two decades. In the coming years, two issues will be the most consequential in shaping the Sahel's future: climate change and population growth. Though both phenomena are already affecting the region, scientific projections predict that the challenges will escalate absent meaningful interventions.

CLIMATE CHANGE PROJECTIONS

Climate change predictions for much of the Sahel presage growing uncertainty and hardship. In recent decades, the main effects of climate change in the Sahel have been increasing temperatures and more extreme and variable rainfall. The 2021 Sixth Assessment Report from the Intergovernmental Panel on Climate Change (IPCC) predicts the following climate outcomes across West Africa, including the Sahel, based on an expected 1.5°C (2.7°F) global increase above pre-industrial times by 2040:[43]

- Average annual surface temperatures are projected to increase beyond the global average. Specifically, some studies predict that the Sahel will be up to 3°C to 5°C (5.4°F to 9°F) warmer by 2050.[44]

- Extreme heat and heat waves will be more frequent. On average, children born in West Africa in 2020 will endure four to six times more heat waves than those born in the 1960s.

- Rainfall is projected to decrease in the western part of the region and increase in the eastern part. The western Sahel will experience a four- to six-day-shorter rainy season due to delayed rainfall onset.

- Heavy rainfall events will become more frequent and intense, increasing the likelihood of flooding.

- In higher global warming scenarios—at 2°C to 3°C—the likelihood of drought and the lengths of droughts are expected to increase in the western Sahel.

Although IPCC experts have medium confidence in many of these predictions, weather data from the region remains limited, meaning that such predictions are subject to greater uncertainty.[45] The IPCC predictions indicate that effects are localized, and in some cases appear mixed. Yet, taken as a whole, those changes will likely hurt communities due to increasing variability from normal weather patterns disrupting agricultural productivity, food security, and health.

DEMOGRAPHIC PROJECTIONS

By 2050, it is expected that one in four people in the world will be from Africa.[46] Much of this rapid population growth is driven by countries in the Sahel. In 1960, the population of the six Sahelian countries numbered only about twenty-one million; by 2040 that figure could reach two hundred million. If northern Nigeria, which shares similar population features to those six countries, is included, then this estimate is closer to four hundred million.[47] This remarkable growth results from declines in infant mortality, increased life expectancy, and, most of all, persistently high fertility rates. Within the Sahel, fertility rates range from 4.7 children per woman in Senegal to 7 per woman in Niger—two to three times the global average.[48]

The demographic profile of Sahelian countries will change dramatically because of this rapid population growth. On average, the populations of Sahelian countries will become younger. Across the region, roughly half of the population is now under the age of fifteen; by 2050, the number of people under the age of twenty is expected to double.[49] Urbanization is also likely to increase as households become unable to sustain themselves through agriculture.

The implications of these demographic changes cannot be overstated, even if their social and political effects are ambiguous. A large youth cohort, commonly known as a "youth bulge," could increase the risk of unrest, but it could also lead to human capital gains and contribute to labor productivity and economic growth.[50] Similarly, urbanization could be a stepping stone to development or a path toward more social and political ills, including growing inequality.

FOOD, WATER, AND HEALTH SECURITY

Over the next few decades, climate change and demographic transformations will threaten access to food and water, and the overall health for the most vulnerable communities in the Sahel. A shorter and more variable rainfall season—already observable in parts of the Sahel—will undermine food systems. In particular, an uneven distribution of rainfall, even at constant or higher overall levels, undermines agricultural productivity.[51] For example, in a 1.5°C (2.7°F) global warming scenario, yields of sorghum, one of two major staple crops in West Africa, are expected to decrease by 9 percent.[52] Rainfall variability, coupled with demographic growth, can lead to a sharp decline in per capita agricultural yields for farming households, signaling deteriorating food security in the future.[53] For non-farming households, reduced agricultural productivity can lead to soaring food prices.[54]

Access to water is a vital human need that crosscuts with food security and health. According to the World Bank, about 40 percent of the population of Sahelian countries (excluding Senegal) lack basic access to a water supply, with rural areas the most deprived. As a result of factors including climate change and population growth, per capita renewable water resource availability will decline by 2040, putting countries such as Burkina Faso below the threshold of absolute water scarcity.[55] Water insecurity, in turn, will impair agricultural productivity as well as sanitation and health. In fact, by limiting access to clean water, climate change is expected to cause an additional twenty to thirty thousand diarrheal deaths in children worldwide by 2050; diarrheal diseases are already the leading cause of deaths among children under five.[56] Though surface water is increasingly scarce and sensitive to seasonal climate fluctuations, the Sahel is endowed with a tremendous amount of groundwater in aquifers that, if carefully and sustainability managed, can help meet future needs.[57]

DEVELOPMENT AND ECONOMIC GROWTH

In the next decade or so, agriculture will continue to be a linchpin of Sahelian economies. Efforts to improve agricultural productivity are central to development strategies in the Sahel, especially given increasing volatility due to climate change. Countries have myriad opportunities to expand irrigated agriculture. However, the expansion of large-scale irrigation schemes should carefully weigh the potential economic benefits against social and ecological costs.

In the past, large irrigation projects such as the Office du Niger in central Mali, which is set on more than two million hectares of land in the densely populated inner Niger Delta, have come at the expense of smallholder farmers, herders, and fishers who have been displaced.[58] The construction of upstream dams such as the Fomi and Taoussa dam projects in Guinea and Mali, respectively, are expected to affect downstream water quality and levels, jeopardizing the livelihoods of some one million people who practice traditional farming.[59] Though these projects enable the production of cash crops such as sugarcane and rice on a commercial scale, and reduce the risks of climate-related fluctuations in rainfall, the operational costs are high and the benefits have not been distributed evenly.[60]

Economic development will struggle to keep pace with the rapidly expanding populations in the Sahel. In the future, diminishing opportunities in rural areas will propel many young people toward towns and cities. The development of the region's agricultural industry (including the processing of agricultural products), agribusiness, and mining will offer jobs outside of traditional farming.[61] Countries are also looking to regional market integration to create economies of scale across agriculture and other sectors. The first regional special economic zone in West Africa, which Burkina Faso, Ivory Coast, and Mali established in 2018, is one example. This effort, known as the "SKBo triangle" (for Sikasso-Korhogo-Bobo-Dioulasso), seeks to attract private investment and create jobs across the three countries.[62] Further market integration through regional bodies such as ECOWAS and the newly established Africa Continental Free Trade Area, which is predicted to lift thirty million people out of extreme poverty and increase the income of more than sixty-eight million people across Africa, can support future economic growth.[63]

Economic development along with population growth will have implications for the region's energy needs, which at present are quite low. Currently, the Sahel contributes only 0.15 percent of global carbon dioxide emissions, largely due to low levels of energy access.[64] In the future, however, the dilemma that Sahelian countries will face—as will much of Africa—is how to ensure low-cost and reliable energy access while reducing reliance on nonrenewable sources. To its advantage, immense potential exists for solar power and other renewable energy in the Sahel. However, infrastructure is lacking and will require substantial up-front investments.[65]

INTERNAL AND EXTERNAL MIGRATION

Mobility will continue to be a critical pressure valve for communities in the Sahel facing environmental and economic hardship in rural areas. And climate change and population growth could change the nature of migration from the Sahel. Experts agree that climate change will primarily spur migration within countries. By 2050, West Africa is expected to see the biggest global increase in internal migrants due to climate change—up to 54.4 million.[66] Much of this mobility will probably manifest in the growth of urban areas. Increasing climate variability and overcrowding is likely to prompt more permanent or semipermanent migration in West African countries, as opposed to the current pattern of seasonal migration.[67] Continued urban growth will result, particularly in coastal areas. Cities such as Lagos and Abidjan are predicted to grow by tens of millions in the coming decades.[68] Faced with increased pressure on infrastructure and services, cities will need massive investments and planning to avert social unrest and to mitigate the risk of hazards such as floods.

Concerns that climate and economic migrants from the Sahel will increasingly seek to migrate toward Europe should be tempered by the observation that migration typically is constrained by two factors: social networks and financial resources. Although migration from sub-Saharan Africa to Europe peaked around 2015, driven by the proliferation of smuggling networks and lower costs of travel resulting from the security vacuum in Libya, irregular migration has drastically declined since the adoption of new border management policies.[69]

Even at its peak, migration from most Sahelian countries remained low. Per capita income levels indicate that migration from the Sahel to Europe will continue to be a relatively minor phenomenon compared to regional or internal migration (apart from Senegal, which is relatively more developed and has a large, established diaspora in Europe).[70] The ability of some populations to migrate could also be entirely forestalled due to income depletion resulting from environmental hardship—a situation referred to as forced immobility.[71]

STATE FRAGILITY AND CONFLICT

States' ability to address the social, economic, and political challenges resulting from climate and demographic changes will determine in large part the stability of Sahelian countries. Prioritizing security and equitable development, including expanding and ensuring sustainable access to food, water, energy, and economic opportunities will help address political grievances and avert further violence.

As Sahelian states continue to try to contain and reverse the spread of violent extremist and insurgent groups, new risks to social cohesion are emerging. In communities where government-affiliated forces have been able to regain control, other communities that remain under the occupation of armed groups could be perceived as sympathizers.[72] As such, with the return of displaced populations back into their communities, the risk of intercommunal tensions and conflict is high, absent reconciliation and trust-building measures.

A major challenge to dealing with these delicate and complex challenges in the Sahel is the recent rise of undemocratic regimes, in particular, the suspension of civilian-led, constitutional rule and the emergence of military governments in Burkina Faso, Chad, and Mali since 2020. In Mali, as the United States, France, and other allied nations ended military assistance and engagement with the military junta, the new regime turned to the Wagner Group, a Russian private military company with links to the Kremlin. The group's involvement has further inflamed the conflict, as evidence of human rights abuses and atrocities arise, including the massacre of an estimated three hundred civilians in Moura, allegedly by the Wagner Group and Malian armed forces.[73] While in the past, Western partners have focused mostly on addressing the region's serious security challenges—at times turning a blind eye to governance shortcomings—a recognition that instability ultimately results from "a crisis of state legitimacy" should frame their future policy in the region.[74]

POLICY IMPLICATIONS AND RECOMMENDATIONS

To date, Western partners have largely failed in their attempts to secure stability in the Sahel. Multilateral and bilateral institutions have a strong presence in the region, but their efforts have bifurcated challenges of security and broader resilience, often resulting in a siloed and disintegrated response. As security risks continue to multiply, they have recognized that reducing vulnerabilities by responding to socioeconomic and political concerns is necessary to achieve broader stability goals. A climate security approach that centers on human security—that is, an approach that focuses on the environment's relation to human life and well-being, including aspects of health and hunger—affords the greatest opportunity for peace and resilience in the region.

SHORTCOMINGS AND LIMITATIONS OF APPROACHES TO DATE

Since the 2000s, the focus of external policy in the Sahel has been to curtail the spread of violent extremism. As early as 2005, the U.S. government established a multiagency, multiyear effort known as the Trans-Sahara Counterterrorism Partnership (TSCTP) to assist countries in North and West Africa to combat terrorism. The occupation of northern Mali by violent extremist organizations (VEOs) spurred an expansion of international military responses, including the establishment of the United Nations Multidimensional Integrated Stabilization Mission in Mali, the deployment of a French counterterrorism force called Operation Barkhane, and a European Union contingent termed Task Force Takuba, as well as other foreign troop mobilizations.[75] At the same time, military and security assistance has continued to flow to the region to strengthen state military capacity and to create a new regional counterterrorism structure, the G5 Sahel, consisting of Burkina Faso, Chad, Mali, Mauritania, and Niger.

Despite these efforts, insecurity in the Sahel has increased, with the number of violent incidents rising eightfold between 2015 and 2020.[76] Multiple factors have contributed to this trend, including shortcomings of past policy efforts. For example, though the TSCTP has evolved over the years, it has failed to live up to expectations, facing challenges with interagency coordination, mismanagement, and a lack of evidence in achieving its stated outcomes.[77] A core problem with TSCTP has been its substantial investment in military assistance and security, with relatively less to show for addressing structural drivers of conflict.[78] Similarly, the presence of armed forces has not translated into success against VEOs, as national and foreign security forces have been implicated in abuses against civilians, significantly undermining their ability to win popular support.[79] Failure to address those abuses, as along with broader governance failures, has played to the advantage of VEOs that capitalize on the frustration of civilians, on whom counterinsurgency measures have taken a heavy toll.

In comparison with security and stabilization assistance, investments in development—especially those focused on climate adaptation —have fallen short of the region's needs. In terms of climate finance, the UN Framework Convention on Climate Change established the principle of "common but differentiated responsibility and respective capacities" of developed countries to provide financial resources to assist developing countries in mitigation and adaptation efforts.[80] Resulting from this principle, commitments such as $100 billion annually in climate finance for developing countries by 2020 were made, but have not been honored.[81]

For the African continent, where the effects of climate change and the resulting needs are high, climate finance flows for adaptation are billions of dollars short of the estimated needs for immediate climate change threats.[82] Regions such as the Sahel have been particularly shortchanged, as climate finance tends not to reach the most climate vulnerable and fragile states. Examining climate finance flows to the Sahel and Horn of Africa, researchers find that "the more fragile a country is, the less adaptation finance is received," with more than half the countries in the two regions receiving $2–$13 per capita in climate finance funding in comparison to the average of $18 per capita for all least developed countries.[83] Although preferences vary by institution, generally speaking, donors' low-risk appetite for investing in insecure contexts with weak accountability mechanisms has influenced climate finance distribution. Consequently, fragile, conflict-affected countries are less likely to receive support, deepening environmental vulnerability and perpetuating climate security risks in the Sahel. Further, the climate financing that has been made available has focused primarily on mitigation, while funding for adaptation has comprised a much smaller share: in 2018, only 20 percent of international climate finance was for adaptation measures.[84]

Conflicts and disasters in the Sahel have created a complex humanitarian crisis. Due to insufficient and ineffective development and security responses, humanitarian demands continue to balloon. The United Nations estimates that in Burkina Faso, Mali, and Niger, 14.7 million people required life-saving assistance, including food aid, at the beginning of 2022.[85] Despite the growing challenges, humanitarian funding for the Sahel has consistently fallen short, with only 41 percent of the funds required by the humanitarian community provided in 2021.[86] Donor fatigue in the region could deter bilateral partners as new crises and priorities arise globally. Yet, the risk that instability in the Sahel will expand security challenges, violent extremism, and humanitarian needs in the region—and spillover to others—is too great to ignore. In recent years, groups affiliated with JNIM have started carrying out attacks in other West African countries including Benin, Ivory Coast, and Togo. Operating mostly in border areas where pastoralist groups such as the Fulani have lost access to land and face constraints on pastoral mobility among other livelihood threats, VEOs are poised to replicate their successes across the Sahel in littoral West Africa.[87]

WAYS FORWARD: RECOMMENDATIONS FOR CLIMATE SECURITY POLICY IN THE SAHEL

To date, efforts to address climate security challenges have been reactive; yet climate security fundamentally requires a focus on prevention. Policymakers concerned with supporting stability, recovery, and resilience should consider new ways of working with regional partners that address structural problems to reduce vulnerabilities to climate change and conflict. These new approaches should address the linkages between climate vulnerability, state fragility, and conflict risks, and respond to them in a more coordinated way. The United States has numerous opportunities to shift toward more integrated, prevention-focused interventions including through the Global Fragility Act of 2019, the USAID 2022–2030 Climate Strategy, and the 2022 U.S. Strategy Towards Sub-Saharan Africa (2022) among other channels.

The following recommendations should inform future policy actions focused on addressing climate security risks.

The United States and Europe should prioritize human security by enhancing community recovery and development efforts over traditional military stabilization objectives.

Security discourse and policies tend to be dominated by a focus on state security and militarized approaches. In the Sahel, security challenges are inextricably linked to socioeconomic and governance issues and require a broader understanding and response. While certain parts of the region will require greater military efforts to reverse the territorial gains of VEOs, a crucial ingredient for success will be the recovery and reconstruction of liberated areas, and the prevention of further gains by VEOs. In doing so, Western partners should prioritize addressing the root causes of fragility in the region, including poverty and underdevelopment, weakness in governance, and growing group grievances related to marginalization, inequality, and injustice. These challenges are formidable, and experiences to date should demonstrate that they cannot be resolved militarily. Rather, policymakers should shift funding away from a military-first approach and prioritize fully funding humanitarian, development and peacebuilding needs. The nature of the protracted and multifaceted crisis in the Sahel also calls for less stove-piped aid investments and more integrated responses that respond to urgent needs, strengthen capacities to resolve conflict peacefully, and build lasting resilience to environmental, economic, and conflict-related shocks.

To date, donors have invested billions of dollars to improve security and development in the Sahel, including through initiatives such as the Sahel Alliance, which has coordinated almost 23 billion euros across more than 1,100 projects since 2017.[88] Such commendable efforts should continue, but with a clear focus on peace and development outcomes, rather than muddling these goals with short-term, conflicting objectives, such as curbing immigration to the West, which has perennially been an overarching priority of European donor investments in the region.

The United States and Europe should help facilitate credible governance and the rule of law by partnering with civil society and accountable governments to provide basic services.

Central to a focus on improving human security as part of a climate-security agenda in the Sahel is understanding the role of governance and government policies. Weak and ineffective governance is an underlying source of climate vulnerability, reducing adaptive capacity and contributing to conflict in the region. As such, good governance and inclusive growth should be at the center of climate security efforts. While recognizing that the onus of governance and policy reform rests with the sovereign states of the Sahel, foreign policy in the region should consistently prioritize and support initiatives that demonstrate a commitment to these principles.

Investing in the development of strong, accountable governance institutions and services will reap stability gains in the Sahel. Development assistance should prioritize democracy and governance programming, working with civil society organizations to help articulate a bottom-up vision for the Sahel's future where possible. Further, investments to improve basic services, including healthcare, education, and the rule of law can both respond to citizens' immediate needs and help garner support for responsive governments that provide these services.

Bilateral and multilateral aid donors should overcome risk aversion to ensure that aid reaches marginalized areas and disadvantaged demographic groups.

Violence and insecurity thrive in marginalized communities that lack access to basic services and support from the state. While supporting the development of effective and just governance institutions that can expand their reach and presence in these areas, donors should also provide aid where state institutions are absent. Humanitarian organizations have ample experience working in remote and insecure settings by maintaining their neutrality and a focus on providing life-saving services. Expanding humanitarian and some development work in peripheral areas will require more risk tolerance from donors, who will need to invest in areas that could be near VEO strongholds. Such efforts would benefit from enhanced civil-military coordination, ensuring that assistance can reach marginalized communities while maintaining the safety of aid actors. Working with local organizations will also enable greater access to hard-to-reach communities.

Within communities, foreign actors should mind their initiatives do not exacerbate existing inequalities, but rather work toward the inclusion of marginalized groups. Although they are often overlooked, women and youths are uniquely vulnerable to climate change and insecurity and should play an important role in adaptation and peacebuilding efforts. Women's empowerment and education could also help slow population growth over time. Helping women and youth have a place at the table in local decision-making and working in culturally sensitive ways to highlight the benefits of advancing women's and youths' agency should be mainstreamed within all development, humanitarian, and peacebuilding efforts.

The United States and Europe should strengthen accountability for abuses committed by partner security forces in the Sahel and do more to counter disinformation about their presence.

Despite noted shortcomings of military assistance and other counterterrorism efforts in the Sahel, security actors still need to reverse the territorial gains of VEOs. Development and peacebuilding efforts are unlikely to be effective in the absence of security. After withdrawing its troops involved in Operation Barkhane from Mali in 2022, France has an opportunity to rethink its military objectives and approach in the Sahel. Support for national and regional security forces that have been implicated in abuses against civilians has been the Achilles' heel of counterterrorism efforts. As such, curbing and ensuring accountability for abuses against civilians is necessary to win the trust of communities. Western partners should also recognize the disinformation campaign being employed to taint public opinion of their involvement in the Sahel. As the ex-colonial power in the region, France has been an easy target for deflecting security and governance failures by both the military-led government in Mali and its ally, Russia.[89] Countering disinformation through a clear public communication strategy— coupled with accountability for past abuses—will help build credibility and support for France and allied partners' involvement in counterterrorism efforts.

The United States and Europe should prioritize investments in adaptation efforts over mitigation efforts and remove barriers to the use of natural gas in keeping with local priorities.

While international institutions and donors have committed to financing mitigation and adaptation equally, they should recognize that adaptation finance is the priority for African countries due to their increased vulnerability to climate change and their limited contribution to global emissions. For example, in examining African countries' Nationally Determined Contribution plans—the climate action plans to cut emissions and adapt to climate change required of all parties to the Paris Agreement—their overwhelming focus is on needs related to improving agriculture, food and water security, and disaster risk reduction.[90] To avert the most devastating effects of climate change on economic development, livelihoods, and health and safety in the Sahel, donors should prioritize investments in adaptation.

Moreover, as regions such as the Sahel continue to grow—both economically and in population—mitigation goals should be calibrated with economic development and poverty alleviation imperatives. Energy needs are expected to increase, and while investments in clean and renewable energy are critical, less developed nations like those in the Sahel should not be expected to "leapfrog" to relying only on clean and renewable energy sources such as solar and wind. Rather, as the African Development Bank notes, a just transition implies that regions like the Sahel be afforded "the energy transition and decarbonization policy space and time horizon needed to balance development goals and climate objectives."[91] For example, although some European donors and the United States have pledged to stop funding projects that depend on any fossil fuel, natural gas—which is abundant in Africa and cleaner than burning wood, coal, and oil—should be considered as a transition fuel for the continent.[92]

Bilateral and multilateral aid donors should honor prior climate financing commitments and open more channels for aid to prevent the worst human costs of climate change.

To enhance adaptation efforts, closing the climate finance gap for Sahelian countries is necessary. Highly developed countries should renew and honor their commitment to providing $100 billion annually in climate financing for developing countries. At the same time, overcoming risk aversion to investing in fragile countries and reducing the administrative complexity of access to financing for low-income countries from multilateral aid funds such as the Green Climate Fund can open more avenues of climate adaptation financing for Sahelian countries.[93] Another pivotal opportunity to speed up adaptation efforts is by financing climate-resilient COVID-19 recovery. The UN Environment Program (UNEP) predicts that a low-carbon pandemic recovery could cut 25 percent of global greenhouse gas emissions, compared with policies currently in place.[94] As Sahelian countries and their partners work to rebuild livelihoods, markets, and economies hurt by the COVID-19 pandemic, recovery packages can support mitigation and adaptation by prioritizing clean, sustainable growth and development. Investing in building infrastructure for green energy, climate-resilient jobs and livelihoods, and disaster risk reduction will help Sahelian countries better prepare for the future.

Bilateral and multilateral aid donors should support existing community and regional-level institutions and their locally led climate adaptation and peacebuilding initiatives.

Foreign actors should encourage Sahelian communities' own sources of climate resilience and risk management practices. Yet the pace at which environmental conditions are changing—coupled with the effects of conflict and other shocks—means that these coping mechanisms are increasingly insufficient. Similarly, many systems for managing conflict across the region have broken down. Because local responses have the greatest chance of success, climate security in the Sahel should advance policy options identified and led by communities and their leaders.

In practice, this strategy entails first working with trusted institutions at the local, sub-national, national, and regional levels. Since climate vulnerability is context-specific, adaptation efforts should focus first on the local level. Decision-making and responsibility for resources can be devolved to sub-national institutions to help tailor responses to community needs. One replicable example is the County Climate Change Funds (CCCF), which the Kenyan government created to allow county governments to integrate climate adaptation efforts into their development plans.[95]

At the community level, programs can also strengthen dispute resolution mechanisms and involve formal and informal leaders in peace-building and resource management initiatives. Finally, because of the transnational nature of climate change, cooperation at a regional level is also necessary. Existing institutions such as ECOWAS can coordinate across Sahelian countries on issues such as transhumance, migration, water management, and security. Rather than replicating efforts through parallel structures, actions can be streamlined by strengthening the capacity of ECOWAS to better respond to these challenges.

CONCLUSION

Climate change is already significantly affecting the Sahel, contributing to greater weather variability, extreme events, and steadily warming temperatures. These changes have disrupted livelihoods, food systems, health, and traditional ways of life. A lack of options for coping and adaptation leaves the most vulnerable communities in a position of human insecurity, creating grievances to be exploited by VEOs and other nonstate actors. The future will present even greater challenges as demographic growth and intensifying climate change put more stress on the environment.

Despite these risks, the potential for instability, including continued conflict and displacement, can be curtailed to the extent that Sahelian governments and their external partners respond with timely, robust, and evidence-informed actions. Success will require greater policy coherence and investments in climate adaptation, development, and good governance. Although the most important factor for averting greater instability is the willingness of national governments to prioritize and lead these actions with transparency, inclusiveness, and accountability, external partners, including regional bodies and donors, can also lend their support. A resilient, stable, and prosperous Sahel is realizable through international cooperation for a more sustainable and just global order.

ENDNOTES

1. Thurston Clarke, *The Last Caravan: 1970s in the Sahara—The Natural Disaster That Threatened a Nomadic People with Extinction* (New York: Putnam, 1978), 23.

2. "Demographic Challenges of the Sahel," Population Reference Bureau (PBR), January 14, 2015, https://www.prb.org/resources/demographic-challenges-of-the-sahel.

3. Several analyses also include the twelve Muslim-majority states of northern Nigeria in the western Sahel, but this paper does not, given the different political and institutional features of those states.

4. "Decade of Sahel Conflict Leaves 2.5 Million People Displaced," UN News, January 14, 2022, https://news.un.org/en/story/2022/01/1109772#:~:text=According%20to%20 estimates%20from%20UN,flee%20into%20a%20neighbouring%20country;.

5. Eoin F. McGuirk and Nathan Nunn, "Transhumant Pastoralism, Climate Change and Conflict in Africa" (working paper, Harvard University, December 2021), https://scholar .harvard.edu/nunn/publications/nomadic-pastoralism-climate-change-and-conflict -africa. See also Solomon Hsiang, Marshall Burke, and Edward Miguel, "Quantifying the Influence of Climate on Human Conflict," *Science* 341, no. 6151 (August 2013).

6. Daniel Kangogo, Peter Läderach, and Grazia Pacillo, "How Does Climate Change Exacerbate Root Causes of Conflict in Mali?" (factsheet, Consortium of International Agricultural Research Centers (September 2021) https://cgspace.cgiar.org/bitstream /handle/10568/116312/EA_MALI.pdf?sequence=6&isAllowed=y; Alison Heslin, "Riots and Resources: How Food Access Affects Collective Violence," *Journal of Peace Research* 58, no. 2, (March 2021) https://journals.sagepub.com/doi/10.1177/0022343319898227.; See also Idean Salehyan and Cullen S. Hendrix, "Climate Shocks and Political Violence," *Global Environmental Change* 28 (September 2014), 239-250. https://www .sciencedirect.com/science/article/abs/pii/S0959378014001344.

7. Marwa Daoudy, "Rethinking the Climate–Conflict Nexus: A Human–Environmental– Climate Security Approach," *Global Environmental Politics* 21, no. 3 (August 2021) https://direct.mit.edu/glep/article-abstract/21/3/4/101031/Rethinking-the-Climate -Conflict-Nexus-A-Human?redirectedFrom=fulltext.

8. "The IPCC's Sixth Assessment Report: Impacts, Adaptation Options and Investment Areas for a Climate-Resilient West Africa," (factsheet, Climate and Development

Knowledge Network, March 2020), https://cdkn.org/sites/default/files/2022-03/IPCC%
20Regional%20Factsheet%202_West%20Africa_web.pdf.

9. "ND-GAIN Country Index: Rankings," Notre Dame Global Adaptation Initiative, accessed May 23, 2022, https://gain.nd.edu/our-work/country-index/rankings.

10. "Global Data: Fragile States Index 2022," Fund for Peace, accessed June 10, 2022, https://fragilestatesindex.org/global-data.

11. "Sahel Drought: Understanding the Past and Projecting Into the Future," Geophysical Fluid Dynamics Library, accessed June 10, 2022, https://www.gfdl.noaa.gov/sahel-drought.

12. Camilla Toulmin, *Land Investment and Migration: Thirty-Five Years of Village Life in Mali* (Oxford: Oxford University Press, 2020), 56.

13. Hal Sheets and Roger Morris, "Disaster in the Desert: Failures of International Relief in the West African Drought," (Washington, DC: Carnegie Endowment for International Peace, 1974), 1, https://pdf.usaid.gov/pdf_docs/PCAAB550.pdf.

14. Maha Skah and Rida Lyammouri, "The Climate Change–Security Nexus: Case Study of the Lake Chad Basin," Policy Center for the New South, (June 2020), https://www.policycenter.ma/sites/default/files/2021-01/RP%20-%2020-08%20%28skah%20%26%20Lyamouri%29.pdf; "Drought Desertification and Regreening in the Sahel," United Nations Convention to Combat Desertification, 2021, https://knowledge.unccd.int/publications/drought-desertification-and-regreening-sahel.

15. *Livelihood Security: Climate Change, Conflict and Migration in the Sahel,* (Geneva: United Nations Economic Programme, 2011), https://wedocs.unep.org/handle/20.500.11822/8032;jsessionid=A345E062ECFC17B5EE71A9F107383E33.

16. Tor A. Benjaminsen and Pierre Hiernaux, "The Long and Successful Life of Desertification in the Sahel," *White Horse Press,* January 11, 2019, https://whitehorsepress.blog/2019/01/11/the-long-and-successful-life-of-desertification-in-the-sahel.

17. CDKN, "IPCC's Sixth Assessment Report," 3.

18. Ahmadou Aly Mbaye and Landry Signe, "Climate Change, Development and Conflict-Fragility Nexus in the Sahel," (working paper, Brookings Institution, March 2022), 8,

https://www.brookings.edu/wp-content/uploads/2022/03/Climate-development-Sahel_Final.pdf; CDKN, "IPCC's Sixth Assessment Report," 3; UNEP, "Livelihood Security," 9.

19. "State of the Climate in Africa: 2020," World Meteorological Organization, 2021, 11, https://library.wmo.int/doc_num.php?explnum_id=10929.

20. Elliot Smith, "Record Flooding Hammers the African Sahel, the Latest in a Series of Shocks," CNBC, September 10, 2020, https://www.cnbc.com/2020/09/10/record -flooding-hammers-the-african-sahel-the-latest-in-a-series-of-shocks.html; *World Meteorological Organization,* "State of the Climate," 20.

21. "West Africa: The 2021 Rainy Season in Review," World Food Programme, Regional Bureau Dakar, October 2021, 2, https://docs.wfp.org/api/documents/WFP-0000133543.

22. UNEP, "Livelihood security," 5.

23. CDKN, "IPCC's Sixth Assessment Report," 5.

24. UNEP, "Livelihood security," 18.

25. Toulmin, *Land Investment and Migration,* 60.

26. Toulmin, *Land Investment and Migration,* 75.

27. Florence Boyer and Harouna Mounkaila, "Partir pour aider ceux qui restent ou la dépendance face aux migrations: L'exemple des paysans saheliens," *Hommes & Migrations* 1286-1287 (2010): 212–220, https://doi.org/10.4000/hommesmigrations.1752.

28. UNEP, "Livelihood security," 22.

29. Saverlo Kratil and Camilla Toulmin, "Farmer-Herder Conflict in Africa: Re-Thinking the Phenomenon," (briefing paper, International Institute for Environment and Development, June 2020), 2, https://pubs.iied.org/17753iied.

30. Mbaye and Signé, "Climate Change, Development, and Conflict," 24.

31. "West Africa Land Use and Land Cover Dynamics," United States Geological Survey, accessed August 29, 2022, https://eros.usgs.gov/westafrica/agriculture-expansion.

32. PRB, "Demographic Challenges of the Sahel."

33. Toulmin, *Land Investment and Migration,* 80.

34. It is estimated in 1992 that about 65 percent of the population in the Sahel lived in rural areas. See "The Demographic Situation in the Sahel: Two Times More Inhabitants in the Year 2015," National Library of Medicine, accessed June 10, 2022, https://pubmed .ncbi.nlm.nih.gov/12344772.

35. Tor A. Benjaminsen and Boubacar Ba, "Why Do Pastoralists in Mali Join Jihadist Groups? A Political Ecological Explanation," *Journal of Peasant Studies* 46, no 1 (2019) 1–20, https://doi.org/10.1080/03066150.2018.1474457.

36. "What Have French Forces Achieved in the Sahel?" *The Economist,* February 2022, https:// www.economist.com/the-economist-explains/2022/02/14/what-have-french-forces -achieved-in-the-sahel.

37. Rida Lyammouri, "Mobility and Conflict in Liptako-Gourma," Clingendael Conflict Research Unit, March 2020, https://ec.europa.eu/trustfundforafrica/sites/default/files /liptako-gourma_study-march_2019-web.pdf.

38. Afrobarometer Data: Mali, Niger and Benin, Round 6, 2016/2018, https://www .afrobarometer.org/online-data-analysis.

39. Sahel security expert, interview with author, April 29, 2022.

40. Benjaminsen and Ba, "Why Do Pastoralists."

41. Ornella Moderan, Habibou Souley Bako, and Paul-Simon Handy, "Sahel Counter-Terrorism Takes a Heavy Toll on Civilians," Institute for Security Studies, April 14, 2021, https://issafrica.org/iss-today/sahel-counter-terrorism-takes-a-heavy-toll-on-civilians.

42. Jason K. Stearns, "Rebels Without a Cause: The New Face of African Warfare," *Foreign Affairs,* May/June 2022, https://www.foreignaffairs.com/articles/africa/2022-04-19/rebels -without-cause.

43. CDKN, "The IPCC's Sixth Assessment Report," 3.

44. Rachel Muller, "Family Planning to Combat Climate Change in Sahel," Yale Climate Connections, January 16, 2019, https://yaleclimateconnections.org/2019/01/family -planning-to-combat-climate-change-in-sahel.

45. Toulmin, *Land Investment and Migration,* 208.

46. Alain Boinet, "The Sahel is a Demographic Bomb," *Defis Humanitaires,* November 27, 2019, https://defishumanitaires.com/en/2019/11/27/the-sahel-is-a-demographic-bomb

47. Richard Cincotta and Stephen Smith, "What Future for Western Sahel? The Region's Demography and Its Implications by 2045," Atlantic Council, November 4, 2021, https:// www.atlanticcouncil.org/in-depth-research-reports/report/what-future-for-the-western -sahel/#:~:text=Population%20growth.,fold%20increase%20over%20sixty%20years.

48. Cincotta and Smith, "What Future?"

49. Boinet, "The Sahel"; PRB, "Demographic Challenges of the Sahel."

50. Elizabeth Leahy et al., "The Shape of Things to Come: Why Age Structure Matters To a Safer, More Equitable World," Population Action International, 2007, https://res.cloudinary .com/dhu2eru5b/images/v1630057258/websites/pai2020/SOTC/SOTC.pdf; Justin Yifu Lin, "Youth Bulge: A Demographic Dividend or a Demographic Bomb in Developing Countries," *World Bank Blogs,* January 5, 2012, https://blogs.worldbank.org /developmenttalk/youth-bulge-a-demographic-dividend-or-a-demographic-bomb-in -developing-countries.

51. Toulmin, *Land Investment and Migration,* 58–59.

52. CDKN, "IPCC Sixth Assessment Report," 10.

53. Toulmin, *Land Investment and Migration,* 80.

54. Mbaye and Signé, "Climate Change, Development, and Conflict," 15.

55. Bonzangio et al, "Strengthening Regional Water Security for Greater Resilience in the G5 Sahel," World Bank, June 2021, 2-3, https://openknowledge.worldbank.org/bitstream /handle/10986/35994/Strengthening-Regional-Water-Security-for-Greater-Resilience -in-the-G5-Sahel.pdf.

56. CDKN, "IPCC's Sixth Assessment Report," 8.

57. Matt McGrath, "Huge Water Resource Exists Under Africa," BBC News, April 20, 2012, https://www.bbc.com/news/science-environment-17775211.

58. Toulmin, *Land Investment and Migration,* 89–92.

59. Bonzangio et al. "Strengthening Regional Water," 8.

60. Toulmin, *Land Investment and Migration,* 214–218. Further, a number of civil society organizations have mobilized to stop investment and development of large-scale dams in the region, arguing that they will led to the loss of livelihoods and displacement of thousands. See: Elias Ntungwe Ngalame, "West Africa Hopes New Hydropower Dams Will Cut Poverty, Climate Risk," Thomson Reuters Foundation News, December 17, 2013, https://news.trust.org/item/20131217125940-0yqo5.

61. Olivier Monnier and Abdoul Maiga, "Lowering Barriers for Agribusiness in the Sahel," IFC Insights, last updated June 2022, https://www.ifc.org/wps/wcm/connect/news_ext _content/ifc_external_corporate_site/news+and+events/news/insights/lowering -barriers-for-agribusiness-in-the-sahel.

62. "Handbook on Special Economic Zones in Africa: Towards Economic Diversification across the Continent," United Nations Conference on Trade and Development, 2021, 127, https://unctad.org/system/files/official-document/diaeia2021d3_en.pdf.

63. Landry Signé, "Understanding the African Continental Free Trade Area and How the US Can Promote Its Success," Brookings Institution, May 17, 2022, https://www.brookings .edu/testimonies/understanding-the-african-continental-free-trade-area-and-how-the-us -can-promote-its-success.

64. Ana Rovzar and Arnaud Rouget, "Clean Energy Transitions in Sahel 2021," International Energy Agency, September 30, 2021, 3, https://iea.blob.core.windows.net/assets/eb3f3d0b -5ed8-4bf9-9f27-3855ed2dbbad/CETSAHELlaunch_ENG.pdf.

65. Annie Risemberg, "Solar Energy Brings Promise, Challenges to Sahel Region," Voice of America, December 11, 2020, https://www.voanews.com/a/africa_solar-energy-brings -promise-challenges-sahel-region/6199470.html.

66. Rigaud et al., "Groundswell Africa: Internal Climate Migration in West Africa Countries," World Bank, 2021, 109. https://openknowledge.worldbank.org/handle/10986/36448.

67. Boyer and Mounkaila, "Partir pour aider."

68. Max Bearak, Dylan Moriarty, and Julia Ledur, "Africa's Rising Cities," *Washington Post,* November 19, 2021, https://www.washingtonpost.com/world/interactive/2021/africa-cities /?itid=hp-top-table-main.

69. Peter Tinti and Tuesday Reitano, *Migrant, Refugee, Smuggler, Savior,* (New York: Oxford University Press, 2017); Erhabor Idemudia and Klaus Boehnke, "Patterns and Current Trends in African Migration to Europe," in *Psychosocial Experiences of African Migrants in Six European Countries: A Mixed Method Study* ed. Alex C. Michalos (Cham, Switzerland: Springer, 2020) 15–31, https://link.springer.com/chapter/10.1007/978-3-030 -48347-0_2.

70. Cincotta and Smith calculate that Europe is the primary destination for migrants only from Senegal, of the six Sahelian countries, with a five-year average of 128,000 Senegalese migrants moving to Europe between 1990–95 and 2010–15. Average net migration

flows for other Sahelian countries is markedly lower. See Cincotta and Smith, "What Future?" 39.

71. Caroline Zickgraf, "Were We All Trapped? Reflections on Immobility During a Global Pandemic," *IOM* (blog), October 12, 2021, https://environmentalmigration.iom.int/blogs /were-we-all-trapped-reflections-immobility-during-global-pandemic.

72. Sahel security expert, interview with author, April 29, 2022.

73. Catrina Doxsee and Jared Thompson, "Massacres, Executions, and Falsified Graves: The Wagner Group's Mounting Humanitarian Cost in Mali," Center for Strategic and International Studies, May 11, 2022, https://www.csis.org/analysis/massacres -executions-and-falsified-graves-wagner-groups-mounting-humanitarian-cost-mali.

74. Ena Dion and Joseph Sany, "After Two Coups, Mali Needs Regional Support to Bolster Democracy," United States Institute of Peace, December 9, 2021, https://www.usip.org /publications/2021/12/after-two-coups-mali-needs-regional-support-bolster-democracy.

75. Nina Wilen and Paul D. Williams, "What Are the International Military Options for the Sahel?" IPI Global Observatory, April 12, 2022, https://theglobalobservatory.org /2022/04/what-are-the-international-military-options-for-the-sahel.

76. "Humanitarian Needs and Requirements Overview: Sahel Crisis," UN Office for the Coordination of Humanitarian Affairs (UN OCHA), April 2021, 4, https://reliefweb .int/report/burkina-faso/sahel-crisis-humanitarian-needs-and-requirements-overview -april-2021.

77. "Audit of the Department of State Bureau of African Affairs Monitoring and Coordination of the Trans-Saharan Counterterrorism Partnership Program," Office of Inspector General, September 2020, https://www.stateoig.gov/system/files/aud-mero-20-42.pdf.

78. Kamissa Camara, "It Is Time to Rethink U.S. Strategy in the Sahel," United States Institute of Peace, April 15, 2021, https://www.usip.org/publications/2021/04/it-time -rethink-us-strategy-sahel.

79. Henry Wilkins, "Rights Group Calls for More Accountability Among Sahel Governments," Voice of America, January 13, 2022, https://www.voanews.com/a/rights-group -calls-for-more-accountability-among-sahel-governments/6395897.html.

80. "Introduction to Climate Finance," United Nations Framework Convention on Climate Change, accessed June 12, 2022, https://unfccc.int/topics/climate-finance/the-big-picture /introduction-to-climate-finance/introduction-to-climate-finance.

81. Jocelyn Timperley, "The Broken $100 Billion Promise of Climate Finance—and How to Fix It," *Nature*, October 20, 2021, https://www.nature.com/articles/d41586-021-02846-3.

82. CDKN, "IPCC's Sixth Assessment Report," 16.

83. Yue Cao et al,, "Exploring the Conflict Blind Spots in Climate Adaptation Finance," Supporting Pastoralism and Agriculture in Recurrent and Protracted Crises (SPARC), September 2021, 5, https://www.sparc-knowledge.org/sites/default/files/documents /resources/exploring-the-conflict-blind-spots-in-climate-adaptation-finance.pdf.

84. Mimi Alemayehou et al., "Reframing Climate Justice for Development: Six Principles for Supporting Inclusive and Equitable Energy Transitions in Low-Emitting Energy

-Poor African Countries," Energy for Growth Hub, October 2021, 12, https://www
.energyforgrowth.org/wp-content/uploads/2021/09/FINAL_Reframing-Climate-Justice
-for-Development.pdf.

85. "Crisis in Central Sahel is Outpacing Humanitarian Funding," UN OCHA, January 27,
2022, https://reliefweb.int/report/burkina-faso/crisis-central-sahel-outpacing-humanitarian
-funding.

86. UN OCHA, "Crisis in Central Sahel."

87. Leif Brottem, "The Growing Threat of Violent Extremism in Coastal West Africa,"
Africa Center for Strategic Studies, March 15, 2022, https://africacenter.org/spotlight
/the-growing-threat-of-violent-extremism-in-coastal-west-africa.

88. "The Sahel Alliance," Alliance Sahel, accessed August 29, 2022, https://www.alliance
-sahel.org/en/sahel-alliance.

89. Christophe Chatelot and Cyril Bensimon, "Paris Fails to Counter Russian Propaganda
in the Sahel," Le Monde, May 21, 2022, https://www.lemonde.fr/en/international/article
/2022/05/21/paris-fails-to-counter-russian-propaganda-in-the-sahel_5984236_4.html

90. World Meteorological Organization, "State of the Climate," 31.

91. "Africa Economic Outlook 2022: Supporting Climate Resilience and a Just Energy
Transition in Africa," Africa Development Bank, May 25, 2022, 73-74, https://www.afdb
.org/en/documents/african-economic-outlook-2022.

92. Vijaya Ramachandran, "Blanket Bans on Fossil-Fuel Funds Will Entrench Poverty,"
Nature, April 20, 2021, https://www.nature.com/articles/d41586-021-01020-z.

93. Cao et al., "Exploring the Conflict." 30.

94. World Meteorological Organization, "State of the Climate," 33.

95. Tonya Summerlin, Moushumi Chaudhury, and Namrata Ginoya, "Insider: Main-
streaming Climate Adaptation into Development: Three Lessons from Kenya," World
Resources Institute, September 15, 2020, https://www.wri.org/insights/insider
-mainstreaming-climate-adaptation-development-three-lessons-kenya.

ACKNOWLEDGMENTS

I would like to acknowledge and thank the following experts and reviewers for their thoughtful insights and edits: Aliza Asad, Jana Birner, Tegan Blaine, Natalie Caloca, Adrien Detges, Christian Kreznar, James M. Lindsay, Rida Lyammouri, Leonardo Villalon, and Samantha Wapnick. This paper also benefited from the invaluable feedback of participants at the "Climate Change and Regional Instability" workshop organized by the Council on Foreign Relations and the Geneva Center for Security Policy. Last but not least, many thanks to Paul Stares for his incredible stewardship over this project.

ABOUT THE AUTHOR

Beza Tesfaye is director of research and learning for migration and climate change at Mercy Corps, and a nonresident senior associate at the Center for Strategic and International Studies' program on fragility and mobility. She has researched and written extensively on migration, conflict prevention, and governance in fragile and conflict-affected countries. Her work has been published in the *American Journal of Political Science* and *African Identities*, in addition to media outlets including the *Washington Post,* the *Stanford Social Innovation Review,* and the *New Humanitarian.* Prior to Mercy Cops, she worked on international development, humanitarian, and peacebuilding issues in the United States and internationally, for the United Nations Children's Fund (UNICEF), Freedom House, the International Rescue Committee, and the U.S. Agency for International Development (USAID). In her personal capacity, Tesfaye serves on the advisory board of the University of San Diego's MS in humanitarian action, and the Better Evidence Project, an initiative that seeks to improve the evidence available to donors, policymakers, practitioners, and scholars in the peacebuilding community. Tesfaye received an MA in public affairs and a BA from Princeton University.